TWINE

~~~~~~~~

David Koehn

Bauhan Publishing

Peterborough · New Hampshire

2014

Library of Congress Cataloging-in-Publication Data

    Koehn, David.
    [Poems. Selections]
    Twine / David Koehn.
       pages cm
    ISBN 978-0-87233-177-8 (alk. paper)
    I. Title.
    PS3611.O3626A6 2014
    811'.6--dc23

                2014006611

Book design by Kirsty Anderson
Typeset in Electra LT
Cover design by Henry James
Manufactured by Versa Press
Author photo by Holaday Mason

BAUHAN PUBLISHING LLC

PO BOX 117 PETERBOROUGH NEW HAMPSHIRE 03458
603-567-4430
WWW.BAUHANPUBLISHING.COM

MANUFACTURED IN THE UNITED STATES

TWINE

For my mother, my father, my sister, my sons,
my daughter, my lovers, my love

Acknowledgements

Some of these poems also appeared in *COIL*, winner of the Midnight Sun Poetry Chapbook Contest, University of Alaska.

"Cross Country Skiing" and "Steelhead," *Alaska Quarterly Review*
"Breba," *Apt*
"To Gerard de Nerval" and "There in Timbuktu," *Arabesques*
"The Professor's Wife to the College Boy," *Artful Dodge*
"Drift," "Ms. Yen's Music Studio Summer Recital," and "The Toll," *BlazeVOX*
"Indiscretion with Mannequin," *Birmingham Poetry Review*
"Turning Out the Light," *Bitter Oleander*
"Manes Gossiping, Overheard," *Carolina Quarterly*
"Denial," *Cimarron Review*
"Market Scene" and "Faith Healing," *Confluence*
"The Twittering Machine," *Chain*
"At the Terminal," *Cranky*
"Swimming Laps at High Altitude," *CrossConnect*
"Horses Shimmying in their Paddock" and "Corkscrew Slough with Mosquito," *Delmar*
"The Tattooed Lady," *Del Sol Review*
"Notes from a Lecture on Sterna Paradisaea, or Mitqutailaq" and "Rescue Vehicles," *Diagram*
"On the Fall" and "On the Equinox," *Diner*
"Le Palais du Cheval," *Dream International Quarterly*
"This Story" and "The Graffiti Artist Settles in the Eskimo Village," *Euphony*
"The Water Skimmer," *Illuminations*
"The Aquarium at the Potluck," *Isotope*
"Perishable Gods," *Kenyon Review*
"Filmskimming," *McSweeney's Sestinas*
"Night Lines," *New England Review*
"After a Migraine" and "Cottage at Red Bluff," *New York Quarterly*
"Purgatory," *Oxford Magazine*
"The Windmills of Altamont Pass," *Phoebe*
"Looking for God," *Paumanok Review*
"From a Journal: Dooker's Hollow" and "Above the Ranch," *Permafrost*
"On the Invention of Boxing Gloves" and "What the Village Did," *Poems and Plays*
"The Attempted Assassination of Jules Verne," *Poetry Midwest* and *Maverick*
"Gin: Dream," *REAL*
"Spurge," *RHINO*
"Early Frost," *Southern Indiana Review*
"Shopping at Williams-Sonoma," *SoMa Literary Review*
"The Shallows" and "Under the Front Porch," *Third Coast*
"The Remedy," *Three Candles*
"Communications in Accordance with Article 5, Paragraph 1 of the Agreement on the Rescue of Astronauts, the Return of Astronauts, and the Return of Objects Launched into Outer Space Partial Pantoum," *VOLT*
"The Marking," *West Wind Review*
"Baron's Shed, Mineshaft C," *Wisconsin Review*
"The Town Crier," *ZYZZYVA*

...errabunda regens tenui vestigia filo,
ne labyrintheis e flexibus egredientem
tecti frustraretur inobservabilis error.

—CATULLUS

Contents

The Town Crier

Epilogue

Preface

The Taxi Driver

The sound of the meter
Ticks off demarcations,
Asleep he dreams
Nothing but destinations.

The Tattooed Lady

The Tattooed Lady

When I sleep she's in my ear.
On her side, she is the endless river—
Not a painted rose, not sideshow.
On her throat, Chinese for bird

Aside oracle bones—a net with shaft—
Originally meaning "to capture."
X of the field artillery insignia
Under labeled parts of a bumblebee:

She's the study of all things, the snake
In the sockets of a pale-blue skull.

One might ask what the cursive *Molly*
Has to do with a map of Timbuktu,
Or why the emperor and the dragon sit atop
A few lines of Latin.

One might even inquire as to why
The naked nymph
In the frame of the painting
Has no tattoo.

But everything means
Because it is part of her body,

Even the teardrop of ink
At the left edge of her left areola,
Even this poem. When she sings
The right breast's moon

Signals the shoulder's dove

To spread its wings
And when she sits cross-legged
On my desk, I see a castle

And when she reclines,
Great Solomon's Seal.
Under her hair, the constellations.
On her tongue? A bitter almond

And all the chords of Blue.
She'll sleep with you. She'll sleep with anybody I ask her to.

After a Migraine

Peeled potato,
Backyard damp with rain.

Sliced fennel,
Concentric rings align

On the cutting board.
A wince of anise and the light

Of bitter lemon on the air.
Everything seems sharpened.

The weave and ochre weft
Underlies the kilim.

A grid of linen blossom
Wallpaper, the graph of mauve

Kitchen tile, X.
Breathing this air

Brightens a net, Y.
Celery stalk strings

Curl beside the arc
Of an avocado pit

Toward my seamlessness, Z.
What pinch of garlic, bulb

Flattened under knife blade,
Lights sliced red bell

Pepper in a steel bowl?
Clockwork wheels of tomato

Seep a single seed
Aside crushed black pepper

Suspended in olive oil.

Cross-Country Skiing

In fatigue, the body, disguised by disappointment,
Speaks what once spoken still remains true:
Like the woman asleep beside you,
A rolling horizon
Across
The sweeping valley
Of white sheets, magnetic fields
At the geographic center of motion
Sloping the landscape to the flash of northern lights.

The sky cleaves the mountains where the coyotes range;
Daydreaming about her breasts, I near
Until, unknown, the night
Has crept up behind,
As if
To strike or to stalk
Or to covet, and all goes dark
Over the white distances; the slender
Skis glide, one, then the other, always forward.

Asleep against her, who would not dream of the plains
Between, cold, open distances,
Regrettable, forgivable.
Two continents
Adrift,
Receding west
And north respectively,
The rift between us, an angle done,
A mode of pleasure: breath, snow, and night.

On the Equinox

The streetlights not yet on, the moon not yet risen,
At dusk the porch screen filters out nothing,
The pollen in the air as gritty on the skin as resin;
And the season wavers above the leaning maples.

The grey cast spreads as unevenly as fog
Rising out of the backyard's cul-de-sac.
Yet, being lost to the ordinary clatter
Of the silver and china in the kitchen sink,

Today is always like this, never sinking
Away forgotten, never noted for the antinomy
It returns—the regret for how the new verdure,
So shy, will untwine its mad, delicate fingers.

The moon has slipped through the fingers of the day
Like a rosary bead. No prayer can return it,
But the trees are black, and night folds over
                  Clean and even as a bed sheet.

Steelhead

Over the uncertain stones, back-casting our flies,
We waded, waderless, through the icy currents.

Our wrists using the fly rod to conduct the morning,
Feeling the weight of the four-count measurement

Of air: one, forward with the rhythm of the line;
Two, let the fly float back behind the ear at the end

Of the leader curving into the shape of an S;
Three, let the wrist snap the rod forward like a wand;

Four, lay the fly, the black feathers of Ariel's magic,
Down in the swift eddies of the Grande Ronde.

The pink and silver blade of fish flashes up
Through the green rush of the deepest flow.

The rod bends over as if to pick the river up.
The tip traces a geography only the fish knows.

The line between fisherman and fish about to break,
A diagram of desire's most disastrous passions,

The catch of our limits, of what feeds us—
Of disappointment in the tools we fashion.

The line goes slack—this disappearing act,
Of fish, of fisherman's body, is without slaughter.

Predator, lover, wizard, conductor, only
The legs have gone numb, at one with the water.

Night Lines

Golden eyes specked with dim light of storm clouds,
Vermillion, chilipepper, bocaccio, and cowcod:
Rockfish in awe under the fishmonger's window,

A display of collectibles from the day's catch.
What measures matter? The half cod on the scale
Is never enough for our evening's bottles

Of conversation. Outside, seagulls tear
At a bag of day-old bread. At the village
Bakery, pastry under glass seeps fruit

As if recently deceased. Sea salt's small spurs
Star the filet; the cottage's counter supports
A slanted window where a distant ocean falls

Short of pale wood skeletons of new homes
Along the fern-ribbed path we walked
Where more gulls eyed you with suspicion

And with what I thought was antipathy.
All afternoon the cottage lolls about the field
Full of Chet Baker's and Stanley Turrentine's riffs

And even more rain supposes the songs anchored
To the aroma of dinner. Before we notice,
The sun hidden under storm strata recedes.

The distant squall line tugged by the under-bit mug
Of an angry quillback has taken the light with it.
This morning, from the window of the Bait and Tackle,

You buy a souvenir poster: a concordance of fin,
Eye and tail. Some can be taken with no limit, some
Like the grey speckled kelp we are allowed

But a few. I watch you admire the rare, dappled-black
Back of the green and yellow China. Others
We must return to the water and tell no one,
But what swims away, also swims into view.

The Marking

The scuppernong arbor is fog-thick with fleas.
One bit his wrist, the almost visible sheath swelled.

His walk took almost long enough to remove
The twinge. Dark towns appeared on the horizon;

The evening hatched struck couplings
Of lights. The sweet of silage occluded the sulphur.

Raw-edged, throbbing ripe as the berries, in the window
He saw his wife wipe her lips. Just less than angry

He asked, "What's this? Whose glasses?"
She said, "Everyone blames me, don't blame me."

Who knew? Is the hawk blinded by the tamer?
So, her silhouette moved so while mopping?

The one-eyed moon at zero brings this back
Tonight as she swashes his girdered nerves:

Deliberately wild. When the flesh
Has slacked from her, the suspended

Smell of wisteria, a blanket over the birdless silence,
Reminds us of what lie was almost uncovered,

Of the benefits of silage. Of what sex could never do,
But the flea could, and again has not done.

Above the Ranch

At altitudes where breath begins to fizzle
The stars have pitched their aviary over
The sunset's distended arc, wide then flat.
The northern lights aerosol the night with dazzle
Not even adolescent dreams can match.
There is nothing about today to discover.

There is nothing peculiar about the herds:
The elk, the lowing cattle, the cumulus sheep
At work in fields dim-lit by porch light below;
Nothing brings us delight, not what we heard
About the spring's hasty thaw, not the rendered tallow,
Not standing tiptoe, reaching, as if out of sleep,

For the uncorked bottle of cider vinegar
To flavor the trout with just enough bitterness.
Pisces sparkles, the ages gain for us an evening
As safe, dark tides wave us toward dangers
The scale of oceans. We stand exposed and clinging
To the mountain, uncertain it will not leave us.

Under the Front Porch

The brewery shift is not over, but school is out
And caliginous sky backlights the porch's lattice.
The postman's stiff heels clop like small icy hammers
Up the slat stairs, then the hinge, then the slot's clack.

The man in the grey suit, we spy him through the lattice
As he descends the sidewalk, as if he might sense
We are there. We are patient. What we lack
In experience we cultivate in our stealth.

The tin biscuit box treasures: a cone of incense
To be lit if discovered, cigarettes, nudie cards,
A pen flashlight, a *Hustler*, a miniature stealth
Bomber. The magazine spotlit by flashlight

Highlights our poker games flush with wild cards.
We try to gamble our young lives away. Such doubts
Will never return. The brewery releases headlights
Into the streets. The heart's misled hammer hammers.

The Water Skimmer

…skirts across the pond to impress next winter's
Ice. The small bug remarks signatures in slick

Longhand: ripples of sympathetic majuscule;
Swift, invisible webs; surface tension's

Compulsory figures; brief filaments
Of noiseless gossamer disappear

Into the vacancy of wish and want.
The water knows little of its own devices:

Lapis lily pads, the triple-tongue of bullfrogs,
And the pond's bottle green wake in pursuit

Of the pumpkinseed. This before drought insists
The county's regents unscrew the millpond's vise.

This before they cut from the reservoir
The gorge's naked, swollen oak, unbending

And rude, standing below yet above the pond
And frosted soot's blackened woodstove.

I remember the skimmer stuck in a mud slick
After the winter's blazon of the redhead:

Peeking over the sill of a winter's cabin,
The rip-turns, the sheen just before the thaw,

A girl in white skates with black laces.
My recognition of her grace on the mottled ice,
The strings of crystal lace, the thread of & and &.

The Twittering Machine

> *"Democracy with its semi-civilization sincerely cherishes junk. The artist's power should be spiritual. But the power of the majority is material. When these worlds meet occasionally, it is pure coincidence."* — Paul Klee

I

Turn the crank. In 1879, two bare-knuckled boxers fight the longest championship fight ever recorded. 136 rounds. Nine months later Paul Klee is born. While Klee is in utero, FW Woolworth opens his first store, which fails almost immediately. The intense light! "One eye sees, the other feels," he said. The first railroad opens in Hawaii. In Menlo Park, New Jersey, Tom Edison flicks on his incandescent lamp for the first time just as Klee crowns between his mother's legs. Wack. Churches of the Madonna. John Brahms completes the printing of *Tragic Overture* just seconds later.

Trembling violin,
Tunisian red, box, ripe date,
Ostinato sun.

II

Turn the crank. In 1922, *Twittering Machine* debuts. Canvas scavenged from downed warplanes for mount, the secondary support inscribed with date, catalog number, and title. Niels Bohr awarded the Nobel Prize, for "his services in the investigation of atoms and radiation emanating from them." Steely gouache, gold foil: "On a misty autumn morning, I spread the large, humid sheets of Ingres paper out on the gravel in the garden…." Onto filled Bristol first, then finished. The British mandate of Palestine begins. Oh, what Wallace Stevens said.

Cockles, draws, wheat starch
Paste, foxing stomas, mat burn,
Sun seeped through water.

III

Turn. 1940, the Nazis forbid Polish Jews to travel on trains. Klee is dying, Göring seizes Dutch horses, cars, buses, and ships. Joe Louis defends his heavyweight boxing title 4 times in one year in a sparse 31 total rounds. As Louis takes out Arturo Godoy in his third defense, Klee dies. Bruce Lee is born. Richard Pryor is born. Frank Zappa is born. Pelé is born. Four months later, four kids follow their dog into a hole in Lascaux, France. They discover four 17,000-year-old drawings. Klee? Scleroderma got 'im.

Birdsong parch, poop shoot.
Pick up, drop, note. Ink gears, dew
On papyrus sun.

IV

Turn, 64 years, 4^3, after the debut of *Twittering Machine* a choreographer writes a piece for ten dancers lit by nine projectors based on six paintings, to Gunther Schuller's *Seven Studies on Themes of Paul Klee*. Madonna's "La Isla Bonita" debuts.

Turn, 1879 Einstein is born. Klee is a gifted violinist who chooses to pursue fine art. In 1955 Wallace Stevens, vice president of the Hartford Accident and Indemnity Company and a Pulitzer Prize winner for poetry that year, dies in St. Francis Hospital. Four ways of listening to four birds on a crank. Skin thicker than canvas, stiffer than Bristol. Scleroderma? Caused by stress. The bird fused to its wire.

Walking line sings wire.
Late evening, sunset box,
Four thin birds over fire.

Cottage at Red Bluff

A picket fence, a white border, its shale steeps
Wind-whipped with mosquito husks. Askew, stairs step

Down to a beach of layered scales, the revenge
Of wave-packed shale, its beveled rock avenged

By mendicant winds thwacking the cottage's shutters,
A lopsided shipwreck of picnic, fire, and weather.

The rain's squall line, a distant ghost net. Clank
Go the close-enough horseshoes, "Close enough," we say,

"That is close enough." Against the wave-worn veneer,
Parched on the edge of the water's memory,

The abandoned plow on the beach: figurehead, prow,
Grandfather's wake, unspinning in the undertow.

There in Timbuktu

It might be possible to live in its valley,
Even so, time makes sure the desert
Will eventually overcome us all
Mounding up dunes of sand over sand,
Over mosque and home and temple too.
And then, once gone, a small flower.

It might be possible to eat the flower
Blossoming there. Though in the valley
They harvest poppies they hope to
Sell to the rest of us at war in the desert.
We missed the golden age of sand
When Sankoré and Sidi Yahia stood tall

Next to Djingareyber, stood for the universal
Enlightenment of poetry over power, of flower
Over missile. There is now quicksand
Where the road traveled turns to the valley
And a broken bridge toward the desert's
Gold, salt, ivory, kola nut. A woman, Buktu,

Grazed her cattle there, raised children too.
Time is erasing this peace, the original
Libraries of Islam, scholarly texts. The desert
Of the age, the Harmattan, the red flower
I reflect upon here in Death Valley,
California, far from there: all grains of sand

Contemplated by Tu Fu. Each idea an &
Coiling somewhere, elsewhere, toward Timbuktu,
Toward flags seen from the valley,
Toward Baba the enlightened intellectual

Asleep in a stretch of reddish flowers
Undoing the sand, a tide against the desert.

It might be possible to live in the desert
Despite Afghanistan's rock, and the other sands
Of Samarkand. The unleavened flour
Of flatbread, from Sacramento
To Katmandu, an ingredient shared by all:
From sea, to mountain, to plain, to valley.

The moon-washed deserts of Timbuktu,
The shear wind's sands are spiritual
In nature: a flower forgotten in Death Valley.

Le Palais du Cheval

There it is, a place built with stones
Found on a postman's route. He never wrote letters.
Sheet lightning pulses behind the clouds
As if all things exist elsewhere, even stones,
And I'm afraid, after reading this letter
To myself, of it falling through the clouds.

My notes are filled with the blood of stones,
The trickle-down of dreams: Douanier Cheval dreamt
Of Egyptian pyramids, of the blue mosque,
And other monuments he'd read of in *The Stones
Of the World*. Each day the dream
Grew: a gargoyle here, a trellis there, a mosque.

He mortared an acropolis atop the towers
Of a French château. A serpent becomes
A flying buttress or the wing of a bird.
He leaves a letter and picks a stone for a tower
He'd dreamt of where a gargoyle will come
To sleep, undisturbed by the birds.

Cheval rarely spoke to anyone. And then he died.
Was his afterlife waiting? And the palace?
My notes are filled with a gargoyle's blood.
Oh icy villain, oh thief. No. When I die
I'll note his last inscription: "C'est le Palais
Du imaginaire." For ink I'll use my own blood.

Faith Healing

Brother Myland,
The tenth of March, thirteen years before this lesson
When I heard the coming of God
Was at hand, I thought you meant
Suddenly, like
Glossolalia
On the tongues of true believers. Or that spirit
Would spread the oil of St. Cosmo
Over our delicate thighs
And we'd rejoice
In carnival,
Everyone prostrate to the Lord, as Jezebel
Lay supine in the cooling fields,
Like Astarte. I understand:
A thousand years
Is but one day
To the Lord, and I've waited these long thirteen years,
Your hands steadying the parish,
Fingers puppeting their heads
Which paint crosses
Of grise and myrrh
Into their parched wrinkled foreheads, grainy as wood
Absorbing the swirl of warming oil
Which cinctures faith, or their shame.
But yesterday
I saw a storm
Cloud the darkened chapel with angelic voices,
Rumbling the pipes, the piscina.
A girl hiked her blue-flowered skirt
Above her knees,
Closing her eyes,
And waited to receive your spiritual alms

And the divination of prayer.
My arms waited for her fall.
But she stood there,
Eyes forced open,
Entranced, overcome. And you said she lacked a soul.
She might have been a goat. But no,
Your prayers work the opposite
Of Lazarus,
Dear Lazarus.
You've slain the spirit of souls. Men, not God, hands cupped,
Arms as wings, angel the bodies
To the floor after your laying
On of hands.

Gin: Dream

She had been in his tea-dream, tea-dark:
Eighteen, Punjabi, sugar-butter, naked
On the room's piebald, pig-footed couch;
The brass clock's domed works stuck or stopped.

The empty bookstore window reminds him,
Yes, yesterday he sat reading Rilke
On a stack of Technical Writing books, and yes,
He was sure it had been her, the one he watched

Pass by the cheap magazines, the one who turned.
There, quick wit would've freed the quick need
To call her Bhara and give himself Mulligan.
Instead he read, read, and read more Rilke.

To have whisked her away from there,
To worship with her like a single drumbeat
After steeping in the fanned heat,
Might or might not have saved him.

But his daydream's passage remains a letter
Not unwritten but a letter unsent
And it is his gin that gives him the will
To distance his office window

From the glare of the bookstore's window—
Yes, the oily glass of ice and gin
Rearranges the myth, his disorder.
He is neither Orpheus nor Pygmalion.

The Windmills of Altamont Pass

The hills are the hulls of upside-down boats;
The rotations sprinkler the vineyard:

Herb garden, wine press, fishbones.
Canary date palms spread like an idea of

The rotations: *Sprinkler.* The vineyard's
Tractor tires, now gardens, now sandboxes.

Canary date palms spread like an idea of
An idea about artichokes, and the fields'

Tractor tires, now harvested gardens. Sandboxes
At the center, small castles, their spires—

An idea about artichokes. And the fields
Arc wide under foothills of wine country,

At the center, small castles. Their spires
Oversee the meandering vines, a view

Arcing wide over the foothills of wine country,
The lake's speedboat, the docks' moor

Oversea, other meandering vines, a view,
Over watershed, from wine press, a propeller,

Another speedboat. The dock is more
Concerned with not being a bridge

Over watershed. From a wine press, propellers
Churn black bass into Cabernet.

Concerned with not being a bridge
Between here and there, hill and air,

Turning black bass into Cabernet—
Falling angels? Samaras.

The hills are the hulls of upside-down boats:
The windmills of Altamont Pass.
Herb garden, wine press, fishbones.

Swimming Laps at High Altitude

As the chin, the shoulder, turn for air, the lungs
Pull for sky. Sky doesn't respond. 1 point 1.

Arm over arm, breath, arm through, 1 point 2.
1 point 3. And then it is there, I mean I am there.

The running dream where I sink into the earth.
The pool is rimmed with fennel. Hot dogs burn

On the barbeque. The wind makes a misery
Of the green-plastic AM radio's songs.

The hatchback needs cleaning: the red sand pail, green
Sand shovel, yellow sieve; a bucket of golf

Balls, a tin full of pale fruits, Titleists and Top-Flites,
Wind-drawn aesthetics. Golf scorecards provide

Course maps, create questions. Yesterday,
On the fifth hole, I shanked a 3 iron

Into the pond, a 1 stroke penalty, and finished
3 over. Pintails scattered, the golf ball plunked

Into the water, sank, as in my swimming
Dream, my dream about swimming. I exhale,

Slick pockets of air rush to the surface,
But not me, I sink. I am surprised I can hear

The radio, long after I have actually
Heard the radio. The Red Hot Dateline's 1-

800 Numbers secret code, HOT DATE.
Maybe the vulgar have it right, I know I can

Screw anything up. Complicate any simple matter.
Maybe it is just an accumulated stack

Of smut. Oh to be those dithyrambic organs!
But no, I am but the flag of an idea waving,

Riffling with direction. Incomplete scorecard,
Mixed metaphor, distant swimmer signaling,
This is where it is, aim here. I am here.

The Auctioneer

The Auctioneer

You have all gathered here to bid on what remains of one man's life.
I am not here to tell you when he died or what he died of.
I am here to call out the items though we have but a few,
And the rest of the goods will be auctioned off in unmarked boxes
Which you can bid on by size, by weight, or by whim.
Consider the boxes empty except for what is inside them.

I do all the talking, and I talk quickly, so listen carefully.
Each *going* should not excite you. Do not move a finger
Unless you want to bid. If you so much as twitch
I will call you out as a buyer, and I will make you pay.
Watch my hands, when they turn out to you for bids, offer.
Do not watch my eyes, I may assume your glance means you've bid.

We have a coal-burning stove, two bookshelves, and a filing cabinet
Full of who knows what, perhaps his blueprint for an afterlife.
In these boxes may be his wife's diaries of her illicit affairs
(She died young). Or maybe his journals, which one always reads
Out of fear and curiosity, gambling that each page
One turns to is not the final page or that its date is not today.

Purgatory

And from the dry bed water sprang
Clean as the blade of a knife.
That water could numb John the Baptist's hands—

And the sins he washed away
Would cloud it.
The miners found her purple-nailed and penny-eyed.

Brother, what was she imagining?
At what ripe hour but dusk
Did she give up and throw herself away?

When she fell from the cliff
Did she think herself like Magdalene?
You can answer that question.

The anthracite coal seam
Runs deeper than I can remember
But this is not new news, brother.

We used to drink ourselves
Flood-quick there, and now I go alone.
I go there to drink, to fish.

I bait the hook with a minnow
And wait like a broken pocket watch,
Check it, check it again.

Baron's Shed, Mineshaft C

I

To stop the gnaw of hunger
We'd grab two Cokes
And some dogs from Jimmy's;
The crack of our voices
Against our eardrums—
Syllables clicking open
And closed like Zippo caps.
The shed, rust and wood, grimaced,
A hound's mouth, the leer
Under the eye of the moon.
The conveyor belt, a long black
Tongue, where twelve-year-olds
Once shuffled picking prime
From shale. Just down the road
From Eckley, we hid
In the abandoned shed,
The pine-slat walls patched
With crushed beer cans.
Inside, pinned nudes struggled
Against the wind—voices
Echoed through bone earth.
After our five a.m. paper
Deliveries—the snow, wet
And heavy in the shovel.
Our cheeks splotched white
With cold, when frost bit,
When we had no reason to hide,
We hid in the cavern
Where we were just
The crackle and glow
Of a cigarette ember.

II

In mineshaft C, safe and dark,
Away from the gawking stare of passion

I necked with Linda, until by candlelight
She swelled red like a bruise.

My mouth groping over her neck,
My tongue groping for words.

Two bodies rubbed sore and denied
Like the white skin of a blister.

The back of my throat
Still felt the pulse, pulse

Of the sucking
Even after she said no.

On the cold floor, breathing
Heavy in the dark, wind

Through the pine slats,
I called my name down

Where I'd never gone.
The drumming of my voice

Swelled and returned
From the cavern,

The mark on her neck,
A claim, a bruise returned.

The Shallows

In *The Reckless Moment* the young daughter accidentally kills her middle-aged lover,

Shoving him off the landing of the family boathouse, his body impaled on an anchor

On the bottom. In the shallows, a pleasantly distorted lens on the stones shaped

As all stones are shaped for skipping, granite, soapstone, basalt, Howo Ware.

At this depth, ankle-deep, water-shine barely conceals the mudfish.

Farther from shore the body thaws, the refrain of waving water.

Longing, let's call it longing because it makes time pass so slowly,

Because as distance is laid bare there is nothing else to attend to. The eye

Wings, flutters, settles on you sitting on a stone near shore. A kayak slips

Between us. The speedboats, leaping across the surface of the lake, veer

Far too close. A few handfuls of the bottom reveal a 1936

Bottle of Royal Crown Cola, a bottle of Jamaica Ginger,

An inkwell, a quarter-pint milk bottle, an orange jar of Chesebrough Vaseline.

Wading farther, water-clouding phytoplankton and algae are clarity lost

To insect hatch, grubs and nymphs, also at work on decay.

Olive, burnt umber, white over pearl,

Lahontan redside minnows skitter away from my shadow.

I have sunk in the deep everything that need never be recovered.

Skeletons. Small treasures. Even suspicion.

We eye the pleasure boats on the horizon. We will not tell each other

What we need to say, but the other need never know. A mackinaw

Pinches a mudfish and swims for the deeps, seagulls afloat above oblivious.

Turning Out the Light

Her hands turn the sewing spool like a toy locomotive
Building speed: she tries to stitch the cobwebbed
Dark into the corners of the room.

Her black hose hang over the brass fretwork
Of the footboard. His head rests
In the cradle of his fingers.

The gaslit room softens the air
Around the nightshirt's silhouette
Draped over her.

The air is calibrated
With wicked tiaras of shadow
Ready to be snipped out of the air

Like sewing patterns.
She turns out the light. The light is a thimble.
The darkness sticks its fingers inside her.

Corkscrew Slough with Mosquito

Bair Island's salt flats, crimson from this angle,
Highlight docktown and a ship wrecked
Against the slough's shallow shoals.

Blades feathered backwards,
I am stable but adrift. The concerned herons
Don't take flight. Scull blades cavitate
And stems wrench in the oarlocks.

Defined by what it is not, like a gamma
Particle, wake visible like a spotlight
Back through time, the mosquito darts

Against wind. Not
Longboat, not scow, not kayak, not punt:
A neuropeptide's stretched light
Navigating alpha waves.

Waves, shadows synapse the surface
Of the bottom. Mirroneurons adjust for imbalance
Of left hand over right; as inner ear corrects

For the asymmetry. The body's
Symmetry provides balance but for the lopsided
Human heart. The blurred sun
Against the eye's incidence mirror lights

The slough's map, what's inside
One eyelid. Lying back in bed as a child,
As if falling backwards,

I back-dive into sleep, a scull

Piercing light wind and pull
Into dream. Each 1/10th of an ounce,
Wings beating 50 times a minute: mistimed

Accordion measures taken before and after sleep.
Mosquito adrift, I inspect the wreckage: a cargo ship
Asleep on its side emptied
Of what cannot be bartered for safe passage.

On the Invention of Boxing Gloves

William Kemmler, just before the end, said,
"The band girdling my forehead needs tightening."
And "Well, at least I got along with pantagruelists."
Once, twice, then the chamber was rancid
With garlic, saffron, and butter, sandalwood and sweat.
No, the *Times* reporters
Never got that smell quite right.
His brain and blood hard-baked,
Brittle-black; black-wire veins
Charred; seared skin with blackened hairs.
The judge, the attendants covering their ears,
Prayed to Lent's halos hanging in the shrove trees.
From the base of the electric chair
A liana of smoke rose from his spine

Like a coil of cigar smoke through the ring
Of the last two bare-knuckled boxers,
Tethered, leathered, callused,
Foundering in their knacker's yard.
Both willing to romp a hundred rounds
And be pummeled until their hands broke:
No safety, no protection, only fragile bone
And the glass jaw. So many mouths full of raspberries
For their slackening weave and bob. Hippo-bellied
And bitter, bulbous in their bestiary masks
They await the next fight's new gloves —
More power, less blood, no broken hands.
Their cloaks decorated like embroidered antimacassars.

This Story

After-imagery of our evening, water spilled on negatives,
Some washed away, others splintered intersections of ice

Crossed by ice. You were walking the hill, a child
On your hip, beer bottle in hand. Your face, caught in a car window's

Glass, not in or out, still just long enough
To mark your passage into an afterworld of not knowing, knowing,

Not knowing you—projections of you at ease on the dark
Muskeg of the bed, then asking in the chiaroscuro darkness,

"Look at me. Look at me."
Blue ice has been leached of its salt.

There are stories. A man disappears over the horizon,
In the shadow of his absence a wolf returns.

This story is about that wolf, this story is about that man.
They sit down at your table and tell this story.

Communications in Accordance with Article 5, Paragraph 1 of the Agreement on the Rescue of Astronauts, the Return of Astronauts, and the Return of Objects Launched into Outer Space Partial Pantoum

I

Dark matter has washed ashore....
    Thirteen children waggle in their hula-hoops,
        A shadow hangs over the ring factory of round objects.
            Mr. Secretary-General, should I mention
                Product NGC 4151?
                Product NGC 4151 is flawed.
                    Mr. Secretary-General, I won't mention
                        What the astronaut was afraid to mention.
                            It is a dark matter.
Mr. Secretary-General, I won't mention
    That your son has drowned in nothingness, ideas, and music —
                In bad dreams and the power of sound,
                    Debussy's *Baudelaire*, its brittle opening.
                        Angstroms and sunspots mark it,
                          Mr. Secretary-General,
        Photonic focus on this darkness matters.
      void : setRest (CircularListNode rest)
            Mr. Secretary-General,
                Dark matter has washed ashore...
                  void : setRest (CircularListNode rest)
        A shadow hangs over the ring factory of round objects.

II

Shaped like the campanile,
   Is it a cistern? A time capsule?
    This dark matter is annodated
         Antimatter in diffraction, against Jules Verne's visions.…
          This is not what we are after
           We manufacture slinky black nothingnesses,
             Stored in the Cisterns of the Boboli Gardens.
              You don't understand? I said it is
           Stored in the Cisterns of the Boboli Gardens.
             You know, Ammannati, Bartolomeo.
          You don't understand? I said it is
          "A tended heart who hates the vast black nothingness,"
                 You know. Bartolomeo Ammannati.
                  Nagasaki.
                      In the telescope?
   A rectangular awl, the image of a lion attacking a human-headed bull,
       An interstellar cloud of dust.

The Attempted Assassination of Jules Verne

Coit Tower looms large over Broadway's genteel
Red light district. Sean Penn has parked in front of City
Lights to buy a book for his son waiting in the front
Seat of the Land Rover. Garlic infuses The Stinking
Rose, leaks down the street where a seven-year-old
Chinese girl skips across the crosswalk inhaling
The 40-clove-of-garlic chicken. Down the street
In Chinatown my wife asks a woman in Cantonese
If they kill and clean the pigeon and the guineas
For you. When she was a child her mother would
Bring home scorpion fish from the Hong Kong
Street market and thump the bag on the floor
Until the fish was dead. Is this how we will kill
The live fowl? She tells me her elementary school
Was built on a street next to the main television
Station, her friends lining up to beg for autographs
Which she thought stupid, as it is the audience
That makes the image. "Who buys the tickets?" she asks,
As if this fully explains her position.
Then adds, "Why didn't they ask me for my
Autograph?" I pull a biography of Jules
Verne off the shelf, dive into a passage about
His favorite nephew's attempt to kill him.
The mad child wanted to make Jules famous,
And assassination was his plan. Borges and Verne
Were almost contemporaries and yet I can barely
Imagine them in the same room at the same time.
Borges thumping the floor with his scorpion fish
In a bag. And Verne, bullet lodged in his calf,
Limping towards a war for peace. Last summer
In the place where Starbucks meets Wang Wei on acid
In the Heavenly Garden, I explained to C. D. Wright

That I work on poems for years on end. Time, a filter.
How else do I know if I really care
About the piece unless it manages
To persist? She thought that rather extreme
And suggested a dose of Frank O'Hara.
At dinner, the guinea fowl stinks of garlic paste.

Ms. Yen's Music Studio Summer Recital

In a bevy of little Pans' mouths, a display of recorders.
Over their kneel-down marimbas, each mallet hovers,

Hammers the size of dumplings. I have known these songs:
The *Sea Shanty's* oblong wobblings; a *Sentimental Waltz* gone

Suddenly drunken; a *William Tell Overture* drowned
By a student's unrhythm. In the expansive round

Of mothers and fathers—braced by a not-quite-encouraging Ms. Yen,
Smiling and nodding—I succumb to the embarrassed silence

Nursed by ill-applied devotion, and stories of Hesiod
Visiting his personal muses on Helicon. The small god

Accepting, at the end of his drama, all the false applause
As he believes all the mistimed measures, the pauses

Not endured patiently, the other children's clumsinesses
Were improvements to the ledger the collapsing universe

Intended. The program calls for Ms. Yen to sing "Think of Me,"
Her vaporous voice, her thick accent, a special treat.

Now, an unmistakable child in lederhosen, a style
Only a mother could love, dangles his toes over the pedals.

What a small figure the memory of ourselves strikes. The black
Bench conveying up the reluctant boy aside a black

Wave that is the grand piano. For the wind, the summer
Hints at the skylight's angles. Ms. Yen dims the dimmer.

A row ahead two girls fire their fingers in unison
Playing rock, paper, scissors: fist, palm, gun.

Market Scene

The butcher smiles, he crosses his arms over his chest, then waves, leaving
      handprints like tattoos on his biceps.
Beneath the glass the brownish steaks like ponds on pastures of pink ice wait to
      be bought for dinner.
Six goat heads frown at passing tourists looking to spend their foreign currency.
Their faces fall, or flush, after finding such unimaginable delicacies, and pass by.

The seafood vendor sips a tall glass of Campari which stains his teeth,
And he too smiles. He picks up an oyster and smashes it down. "We sell good
      food," he says.
With a few snaps of his finger he flicks the shell clean from the pearly meat.
The slabs of squid on a beach of blue-white ice finish dying.

A woman dressed in a black sheet which she's wrapped into headdress, shawl,
      and skirt enters.
Brisk as a dash of ink she barters, buys, and leaves with a chicken dangling at
      her side.
The mouth of the market opens into a sunlit street
And tourists pass as quickly in as out like so many misled Jonahs.

At last, a woman from elsewhere, hanging on her husband's arm as if it were a
      hook.
The fresh scent of everything stews in the heat. She holds her nose.
They pass whole orchards of strange fruit but don't buy and she wonders
With her short, sharp glances sudden as blows, "Why have you brought me here?"

They pass rolls of dates round as logs.
They smile, she eats one, looks into his eyes, they kiss, it is infested but sweet.

The Remedy

The whispered gas told her when to light the stove.
The crown of blue flames nettled
The hull of the skillet.

The aroma of frying snook in basil
Clips the scent of rose from the air.
The bread absorbed the red vinegar

While the vines crept up the lattice.
She watched the match burn down
To the nub—the quick whip of her breath.

Drift

A swarm of blue dragonflies
Bend river over the hemimetabolous iridescence
Of their eyes. I point out the oily-cloud of the burble
To my daughter who wants to know "Did you bring
Your cell phone?" Water clear enough
To point out the river's trout, I think of the spider
Found in the washcloth this morning;
How Anna's hummingbird at dawn hovered in the drainage.
Cliff sides collapse around us like lost ruins —
Granite's jointing into slabs and columns.
She departs for the other side of the world,
Soon. She will promise to call. I recall
What she told me, You are your ringtone,
So choose carefully. Mayflies, the latest hatch
Squirrel around a partially submerged torso
Of a dotterel's fallen willow roots
The tangled bust of some ancient river god
Waiting to snag the unwary.
On rivers like these, I think of a lost friend,
How he would study the 50 varieties of caddis fly
So he might tie himself, in his own way, to the river.
I think of his newborn daughter, "but a grub."
What Greek tragedy lurks in the currents?
Molting crayfish gaze up at us, reverent
In widespread awe of their new skins, claws raised
In praise of their Olympians; my daughter, a reverie
Of Cybele, drifting over her subjects.
At the oxbow, we dismount. Atop a thicket
Of aspen the yellow hood of a western tanager flashes
Amidst the green hearts of the cottonwood.
Three ducklings skitter towards cover, bobble.

Manes Gossiping, Overheard

I can never remember when any of them are.
I see the two of them as getting along
In the long term—though even love is feeling

The pain of that theory. Across several folks
I talked with the idea: this small thing could turn
Into a larger, more positive force if we

Get more involved. *Hidden* is a great word.
I'm not sure it could have been any other way.
Shhh, they hear our voices coming from somewhere.

We know you are there. Yes, I slipped the real estate
Deal from Ohio into your dreams last night. Yes,
The Delta flight from Cincinnati was eventless.

That's our nature, you can only try to direct things
Your direction; but the greater community
Makes it happen: the bottle cap under the bare

Foot, the snake in the rafters, the chance meeting
Of lost loves discovering in each other's stories
How the gnarled roots of the alder aside the sidewalk

Overgrew and confused the yard and the skeleton
Of a bicycle, their conversation turning to the vinculum
Of what they call their fate, turning to the question

Of how to unsnarl themselves from the grip
Of two decades. Keep your eyes peeled for little things.
Typically, we point this out to you, incident by incident,

And you reply We're evolving as fast as possible.
The issue is not that you are pointing to nonexistent problems:
The issue is that your diction and phrasing indicate

A disdain, real or perceived, for your own desires.
We have a reverse tenure system, the newly dead
Have the most pull. I don't expect you to understand.

The veterans are queued up on the return shuttle. Tell
Your friends to wave hello to them on their way here.

At the Terminal

What is in an average suitcase,
Other than 35 cubic feet of space?

What would happen if suitcases came
First-come first-serve to baggage claim?

Who would end up with their own?
A man might arrive back at his home,

Open a bag, and find a shaving kit,
A thin white sisal rope, a black slip,

A star spinning in a snowy
Chamber, a yellow chickadee

Wind-up with a red-hot stuck
To its head. He might pluck

A plastic compass from the pocket
Of a pair of jeans, set it aside a locket

For his wife—slip inside 35
Cubic feet of space—enough for any life.

The Toll

Radio 94.3 plays The Police then interspersed

94.3 plays sound bites from Svengali.

All the while, 10,000 feet above the mountains

My children return to their mother, earlier

A tall writer read a short story about the Himalayas,

As a hummingbird nectared the lilac at the podium....

As a hummingbird nectared the lilac at the podium....

The radio's pentimento ends with my car's

Approach to the toll booth, where there is moon,

Then fog, then fog under moon. No coin for the toll.

Elsewhere, always, elsewhere, a girl picks up

The phone, I write "The phone" and my phone rings.

It is work. She leaves a message, says, "Hi! We're here."

Some Chiclets piled on top of coins in the ashtray.

The cityscape glitters at the far end of the bridge.

Yeti, DJ, hummingbird. (It is catching up to me

Now…from the same distance, the train sounds

Louder when approaching than when it has passed.)

Why can't I pay what I owe? The toll man says,

"Don't worry; I have all the time in the world.

Don't worry; I have all the time in the world."

Rescue Vehicles

This one rushing to the hospital like a giraffe.
This one to put out the fire of embers older than the known universe.
This one constructed of levers and pulleys enabling you to pull the tramp
        steamer out of the river all by yourself.
This one to calculate the grains of sand it takes to fill the universe.
This one to ascend the towers of Syracuse and save Archimedes from his mis
        timed final words and the tip of the angry spear.
This one to arrogate the feather for the 12th-century prayer supplanted by a
        monk recycling the pages by a scraping and a wash to be turned into a
        prayer book.
This one for the palimpsest of math under invocation.
This one for life's jaws chewing the nib of Red Man tobacco plugged in a
        cheek on a distant river fishing with a distant friend, my grandfather.
This one to remove the manuscript from the library.
This one to call my mother the day the plane crashed into her office at the
        Pentagon.
This one to microfiche the *New York Times* article about The Method
discovered by a Greek theologian.
This one for a pilot's license.
This one for unbinding the Archimedes palimpsest and discovering the lines
        in the binding.
This one for words recurring in an eye for the first time.
This one for blueprints of buildings.
This one for diagrams of thinking.
This one for the missing lines on the page discussing the rules for dealing with
        infinity reappearing.
This one for what the television could have become.
This one to weigh the curved shapes of bodies: sphere and cone equal in
volume to cylinder.
This one for the man dressed in black rushing into an exploding room.
This one to carry a kidney to Tuscaloosa for a father of three as if a part of each
        of us has always belonged to other people.

The Town Crier

The Town Crier

My job? To invoke histories, to warn
Of the sheltered lake's thaw.
To blame the eccentric hag

For witchery. To announce her spells:
Do not wrap dumplings in paper.
Do not follow the river—let the river follow you.

Take the tree from the sapling.
Only use ink on invisible wood.
Learn to dance the magpie's steps,

To mimic the parrot fish.
I dress down mannequins,
I provide instructions for seduction

Of the sexless. The mayor tells me
What not to say,
So I've learned enough pig Latin

To inform friends and family
Of the sinking ship, the dam's rising
Waters, the latest affairs, the best songs.

The milliner's daughter fitted my shoes,
Measuring me from knee to thigh,
So I untied the bow in her bonnet

And licked her gold tooth.
Her father brought up charges.
That day I was sick. She paid.

What fun I had announcing
His bankruptcy. I was almost sad
To announce the sale of her horse.

Looking for God

Last weekend my youngest daughter
Watched my son leafing through
The encyclopedia

To find the first president
Of the United States.
Yesterday, she said, "I want

To look for God." I tried
To explain how God was like
An atom—that he was energy

Creating everything
And everyone in ongoing
Processes of physical

And metaphysical
Existence. She said,
"No, in the pedia book..."

She pointed at the encyclopedia.
We looked for the volume containing
God. Labeled "GEOG-GRAN"

It contained GOD including
A black-and-white of Michelangelo's
Fresco atop the Sistine Chapel.

"According to the ...pedia,
Honey, there are four proofs
For the existence of God...."

She would have none of it.
She was far more fascinated
By the picture of an ox cart

Caravan in the GOBI Desert.
And the curved horns of the bezoar
GOAT, and what delight she had

For the tawny frogmouth, a GOATSUCKER.
And then she was done looking
For God. The television

Blared on to Bugs Bunny rattling
Daffy. The hum of my
Computer buzzed its electronic

Dreams, my son knows George Washington
Is the first president,
And my youngest daughter found God
In the encyclopedia.

Horses Shimmying in their Paddock

A coyote crosses the road. A first for me, I slow
But he does not escape beyond the spray
Of my headlights. He stops, he stares, broadside, stiff.
He looks into my eyes. Am I seeing or being seen,
The object or the lens? I am worried a car
Coming from behind will startle him and I pull away,
Trying to catch his profile in my rearview mirror.

As if to catch him was what I was really after.
Not quite wolf, not quite fox, not just coyote either.
Later, eyes sore with smoke, I douse the fire
And travel through the dark to my tent. I stumble,
Overestimating my night vision. What do I know
Now that I did not know then? That this is my
Dark territory, the thick char of burnt pinecones

Hanging in the air. A dream like campfire
Smoke wafting in the breeze. A dream like woodrat
Scuttling down a drainage. Someone pumps the well,
Calling it all up. The brush awaits, I lope
Into the thicket of juniper at the edge.
This morning the Steller's are intolerable.
To my surprise the campfire is still smoldering

A liana of smoke up through the pine.
All the doors are locked, and everywhere I look
I see coyote: that stump; the child's mattress
On the side of the road; the horses shimmying
In their paddock, nervous; the loam on the valley floor.
More Steller's, in their Mohawks, squawking, squawking.
I don't see coyote anywhere. I look, because

I overestimate my good fortune. Is there a new lesson
I've learned about where to look, or how?
Back on the mountain I build my next birdcage.
I rub my eyes still thick with smoke and sleep.
The dump truck beeps in reverse. Jazz alights
Over the Starbucks transom. I notice a shooting star,
A dark-eyed junco, and I cage them too.

Spurge

"Leafy spurge reproduces readily from seed dispersed by explosive ejection from the seed capsule. The plant can expel its seeds to distances of 15 feet…"

I can make milk from burning spurge! From its milky white sap, from this grass not even a cow can eat. There are studies upon studies about preserving micorrhiza…its cortinarius globuliformis with abundant attached mycelium. This highfalutin' mother earth network, this interconnectedness of all things. Yada, yada, la-di-da, blah, blah, blah.

Last year I found a picture of your sister on a porno site. You asked, "What were you doing looking at a porno site?" I didn't think that was really the point. But what of spurge? Avoider of micorrhiza. Humble, peripatetic, its alien umbels sprouting in Wisconsin, then Indiana, Ohio, North Carolina, Pennsylvania, Florida, Germany, North Africa, Alaska, Japan, California. How it gravitates to disturbed areas! This limber weed, this first to bloom, its leaves of bluish-green hues, bracts of flagrant yellow, is at the edge of our property, just beyond the driveway in the cracks of our walk, the garden border, untrimmed edge of the fence. On top of the mailbox. We study its eradication, this hitchhiker, this vagabond.

At spurge.com I get redirected to spunk.com. It is its own economy. Millions of dollars spent at its expense! I admire its ferocity, it pops up everywhere. Its pedestrian capitalism going deeper, lasting longer, firing its seed fifteen feet. Who knew? Its toxin damaging the feet of horses from freshly mowed stubble during haying. Only little Pan and his goats can survive on this juice.

This is the story of sex and my sister-in-law. This is the story of my self. This is the story of making milk from burning spurge, of planting seed just about anywhere. The seed stays good for seven years.

From a Journal: Dooker's Hollow

They call me hunky in the Furnace A.
My window frames the Mala Fana resting
On the charred hill, nestling on my sill
Like an idle armadillo curled in sleep.
Carnegie shipped its two five-ton converters
From Little Bay de Noc to Port Donora.
Nearby, the railers watch the rolling mill
Spit out the bundled bales of blackened rails,
The derrick bludgeoning the hoary dusk.
In the gorge the barren storage sheds leak barley
Down forty-five-degree back yards on Falkon,
To Halket's row of shacks and bow-legged houses
On Pinsky Avenue. On Cherry Alley
We pass the Mason jar of muscatel.
One year ago, near here, they buried Tom.
(My fingers slid the boiled skin from his cheek
Like a wet label off a liquor bottle.)
On November 3, 1851.
I think what I like, but try to keep my mouth shut.

Plaid shirts and bowler caps—the men and women
Curl in the sucking mud on mattress skeletons,
The wire as rusted and charred as the wellhead's lever.
Or they kneel by the smoldering anthracite, the coals
As luminescent as chrysanthemums.
The glowing petals of sycamore ash diffuse
Above the bicycle rims and cinder barrels.
Mary steps past a busted cot to place
The grass-green perch, copper-scaled carp, and chubs
On the iron grate, the starved gills hissing smoke.
Inhaling butter and scallions, I'm reminded
Of what a paradise the hollow is

Or what a paradise it can become.
Mary slides into the conversation:
"Micha is hacking up her catarrh again,
Why haven't you told her? Tell her. Tell her
Boiling the river water will not help."

What the Village Did

The fishwheel turns, turns, empty of run,
With the facility of a windmill.
With white cheesecloth for windows,
Sod roofs sag under the weight of winter snow:
The stern-wheeler steamboat *Sam* has not arrived
With merchandise of dogs, steel, women.
The telegraph taps like a woman's small
Elegant feet across an open ballroom.
With the news the Han begin to eat their dogs
To save their salmon. She dances across the air.
The miners admire her extravagant slips of silence.

The laughing bears are licking their lips,
Spring carrion! The moose and caribou
Hightail it out of the slough beneath
Elbows of black spruce. Her foot dips,
Dances, and men break into tears. Shopkeeps
Nail shut the window boards against looters.
The village chaplain drinks the rest
Of the holy wine while smashing piano
And cross; he guts his featherbed
And fills the church's bell with feathers
And calls the quiet a thimble full of angels.
Judge Wickersham destroys his gavel
But eats his gun. The winter to come
Will never end: the mushers' dogs
Howl at the strips of dried king salmon
Slapped over racks like red wool socks.

The Graffiti Artist Settles in the Eskimo Village

The churn of planes arriving, departing, behind, ahead of schedule
Reminds him of the overpass over his house at home, his house's
Wood slat windows warped just like all the village exteriors.
But while the CB and VHF antennae speculate upon the empty
Air he recollects the stands of TV antennae lining the rooftops of home.
Clear of ice, early August's first waves crash home on new sand.
All this blank canvas: wood slat houses in need of murals. Banks
Of snow needing sundogs. The recently articulated, whitewashed
Jawbones of a sixty-foot-long bowhead whale ready for tattoo.
When LA arrives in the bush, it's all over. The summers are longer,
Now, probably due to the fluorocarbon's aerosol.
The graffiti artist defaces nothing, marks no territory
For there is too much of it. The Chicanos, the Flips, the Koreans,
The Japs, the Indians, the Serbians—they'll ruin the blood
And bring in the Swedish, they say. Exteriors run parallel
For him, but he sleeps soundly in the most beautiful of rooms:
Couches stuffed full of down, and sleep, and money.
There are 120 cable channels, more than he could have afforded,
On his very own TV. The rusted car at the center of the hotel's picture
Window has become a zebra. A dappled sweathouse: his Kandinsky.
The string art of a drying rack: his Pollock. A tool shed: a tundrascape
Scribbled with a herd of caribou. A roof is shotgunned with stars,
Like a mirror of sky, lit with gray blacks, purpled night, the aurora.
He is beginning to recognize the quality of the local interiors,
A lesson he has only begun to study and not yet learned.
His only competition is the dyslexic squiggler who splattered
The misspelled "slat and pepper" on the side of the connex
He later painted to look like a horizon lumped with clouds, a small camp
—With twenty old squaws hung up out front—in the foreground.
What once was rust or just base is now camouflaged against sky.
An elder once mistook it for a box full of heaven—

Nothing but aluminum cans inside.

On the Fall

The flame's bud did not bloom all last summer,
And the empty bank knows the first returns,
A river receding which disturbs its bank's soft silt,
Early horsehair, alders: sparse, gangly, erratic.
The wild rose will not bloom for it is my desire
Which mimics the fireweed's success, the willow's
Incantations. Come, come, asks the river as silt
Disguises the disorder of the current, allowing
Escapes, hangovers, snow.
                              Divining rod, quartz,
Foxtail, I call to her:
Not the first Greek goddess you think of but the next.
She flows downriver toward a small cabin where
A man and his lover watch cattails twitching seed
To the wind. Her love is the current; his love, silt.

Notes from a Lecture on Sterna Paradisaea, or Mitqutailaq

The Eskimo name,
    Middle tail feathers.
        Of feathers
    Into a fine point,
Scribblings
    Amuse and delight
        Even the resident
    At the recorded
Yet there is a stoic fury,
    Evident each time
        Away from
    Was of utmost
Could match
    Turn for turn.
        Ecstatic control
    And who knew
Would cover
    To pole.
        To catch one
    This darting
This uncertain
    Are the secrets
        Half snow,
    Skirmish
According to the film:
    Birds of night
        The arc, hover,

Mitqutailaq,
    Vectors of cirrus,
        suggests a Y
    and then given wings.
on the sheets
    the dilettante
        ornithologist
    antics of one tern's
which stops short
    the tern decisively
        an ill-chosen bluff,
    importance.
this cold-hardy fellow
    Even the scientific name
        of flight:
    such simple
vast territories
    It is, reportedly,
        preening,
    only as quick
certainty,

    half earth,
    with the Arctic tern
black and white
    and water, day
        and dive

notes the absent
    the angle
        drawn out of thin air
    The tern's
of invisible wind
    birdwatcher—
        shrugs and smiles
    airy doodle.
of abandon,
    swoops up
        as if where to alight
    No bird of paradise
for grace,
    suggests
        hesitant, serious, joyous.
    expressions of flight
as they migrate from pole
    most rare
        as if such wicked ablutions,
    as the eye can follow,
this missing middle,
    to happiness.
        the ground's spring splotches
    in standing water.
conceals
    will highlight its flight:
        a single calligraphic swirl.

Indiscretion with Mannequins

The camphorous smell of must and sweat and paint
Fills the jet moth of her nostrils. Her wiry shock
Of black hair, the smears of rouge absorb the light.

Her rachitic knuckles crack.
She clutches her head, a porringer for the mouth,
Under the hissing of flickering spots.

He poses her on her stomach and then spreads her legs
And throws her skirt up past her waist.
The lights are too bright and she falls asleep.

The pencil shades the corners
Of him, in front of a mirror, stenciling his own frame,
The half-moons of his nails glow into his fist.

Her curled toes cling to a filament
Which stretches between moon and planet.
She wakes, her eyes darting

Until she realizes nothing has happened,
And her cheek, flushing beet as if after a bath,
She dents white with fingers not quite her own.
She waits a long time before she makes up her mind to go home.

Denial

Wall clock ticks degree to degree.

Waking to anger dissolved in coffee,
December remembers snow covering
Yesterday's mistakes.

What resembles infinity:
Divining powder shapes
Valley's edge, ranch's range,

Chinook down canyon walls.
Unwilling to be happy, nothing
Sweetens dawn.

Watched until boiled,
Water in woodstove's kettle
Steeps. Yesterday, knots

Thick in pine trunks
Would not split. Elegies measured
Not by snow depth, but by vague

Drafts, cold air shivering sills.
Shunned dreams purl
Along footboards. Nudge

The attic's empty rocking chair.

Early Frost

I   Winter Dawn

We are not here. The sun glistens
On the sandbox sand gone white
As the moon—which is never enough
For our lovers. For our lovers,

The nightshirts and the clothespin
Bag, limp on the coat hanger,
Have frozen stiff on the lines
Strung like mute telephone

Wires across the hoary yard.
The swing set, its skeleton
Swirled with the red-blue
Of a barbershop post, grazes

Next to the tin workshed: the lip
Of the padlocked door wrenched
Just wide enough for the cat,
Always unnamed and uncared for,

The same grey cat, or another,
To slip through.

II   Spring

For us this winter was not just winter,
But a winter as round
And sore and watermarked
As a red ball found forgotten

In an abandoned sandlot.
For our lovers, our distant selves
Hung out to dry, the clotheslines remain
Stiff, the clothespins waiting

All winter to rust. The nightshirts
Will never thaw. The stray cat
Has maneuvered into the house
Where not even the children
Sleep well anymore.

The Professor's Wife to the College Boy

Let someone else purchase the towels and brushes
For the crock, the tub, the palette—you must learn
To neglect the reforming urge. A clean towel is worth
Admitting to felicity. If you lick
Your fingers after brisket then you must.
If you fear the denizens of Coney Island—
The women in their Laura Ashley galloping,
Dark-eyed, away from the sinister fedora
Of the blue suit on the white horse—then love
Their hyperventilating tenderness.

Don't trouble yourself to select this one from that.
Note only your brother's blind, cynical leg-pulling.
He claims there is gold and silver, even crimson.
The dwarf is as pleasant as the dumb in conversation.
And after dinner the milk spills in the dark.
Learn not to eat but consume, as I have learned
Of the steer and the poultry. Pick only a few eggs,
About a dozen will be eaten that week.
The buyer rarely buys eggs. And I rarely sell.
But still they come and come by the dozens.

The pervasive smell of piss and manure clings
To the un-orbiting moons of porcelain
Unused but clean as the pitcher's mouth.
The drawer's starched layers of linen gain

Value the less they are laid under lunch's tins
Grimed with the tractor oil or sod's purchase.
Never wash your smock until smeared with distraction,
The turpentine will only thin the desire
For a string of pearls dripping down a black dress.

My husband? Let him furrow the fields,
Just as he did while courting me.

Breba

This road trip, a blastophagic search
For inflorescence, for internal flowering.
Think of the first fruit:
Bad figs under fig leaves. Think of Jacob's
Stone under shame.
This desire:
Odysseus' grip on the fig branch saves him.
My history, the world's,
"Fig," on my tongue,
Fig on fingers,
Fig in blood,
A fig for the word "nothing."
Tongue in the fruit's vase,
Say "Optiole," opening for the male wasp during breba.
Siddhartha is there under his tree,
"Hey, Sid," I say, "have you tasted this one?"
He says, "I have tasted nothing, and deemed
It unworthy."
Under the other tree Nick reads page 77
Of *Live Girls* by Ray Garton. More pulp.
"Hey, Nick," I say, "this is all completely fucked.
Fucked, completely." He says, "Beyond hope,
But hope I do,"
He is hidden behind his mask,
"Doubting and questioning, but wishing and wanting."
I linger too long and am left with a smallness.
Good fig and bad.
Left with flesh and more flesh
In my own shelter of unripe figs,
I conspire
To not live up to my own responsibilities.
The tree's hymenopteran eyes

Undress me.
I have no disguise.
Figs split by my tongue,
Their grainy fleshiness
Lubric between thumb and forefinger, are a word's
Licked lips,
Its turned tongue.
Eat them now,
For ripe figs won't keep.
In Condit's *Fig Varieties: A Monograph*
He identifies
89 caprifig, 129 Smyrna, 21 San Pedro, and 481
Common fig varieties: a total of 720.
Some varieties were never introduced; others tried, found wanting,
And discarded. I
Have been introduced, tried, found wanting, and discarded.
In my travels I gorge
On Kahramani
And Barbillone. Poona and Paradiso. Jam
Tongue into syllables
Of Signora and Carabaseta.
Like a beccafico
That feeds on figs I am plump
Stuffed with breba.
Seven risen stars
Configure Corvus—
Praise the mulberry child,
Cleopatra's undoing.
A tardy crow flies by, garter snake dangling.
I wait for the fig bird,
For my untimely bloom.
In the many-titled *A Fig Leaf for Eve*,

Jan Wiley, a Salome, is to inherit wealth
From a family that deems her unworthy.
Under how many unworthy names is flesh exposed?
Desirable Lady, Not Enough Clothes,
Or *Room for Love?* Where Jupiter's
Lightning strikes, the tree's fruit is born.
Rename the movie *Flaming Girls?*
Have we arrived at the Girl and the Fig café?
Figurant to figs roasted
With honey and hoarfrost,
Night is pierced with just-lit stars.
As I eat, I am eaten.
Seams burst: must, vanilla, night jasmine.

Filmskimming

Morning, the wallpaper is from that scene
In Barton Fink's Hollywood flat. Next
To me is a woman, Mimi, from Polanski's film
Bitter Moon. She is his wife. My cock is now
Jean-Hugues Anglade's in Beatrice Dalle, the opening
From *Betty Blue*. Reef, her body

Is the shore, salt-stained, at low tide, the bodies
Of the actors outshone by the scenic
Background in *The Tempest. Only Angels Have Wings* opens
With Grant in baggy shirt, rolled-up trousers, bandana, next
To Jean Arthur. Grant in his huge cane-cutter's hat, now
That is discomfort. I am postcoital. In the film

Smoke, the camera draws down on Keitel, the film
Doesn't cut nor pan as Keitel's body
Holds us to the story of the blind woman. Now
She is telling me a story about a blind woman, a scene
Where a dog leads her into a busy street, next
Cars rush past her, one stops, its door opens.

I ask her if there isn't a film that opens
Just that way. I am James Spader in the film
Sex, Lies, and Videotape. Inquisitor. Next,
Cut to breakfast, I am Stansfield's body
At the end of *Léon*. Or am I Hackman in the film
The Firm, overtaking Tripplehorn? Now

As I lift the coffee to my lips, *And Now
For Something Completely Different* opens
At the table. The bank robber in a lingerie shop scene
Lifts her spirits. The morning light is a gold film

On the day's spot, like the stage from *Headless Body*
In Topless Bar. I don't know what will come next.

Suddenly a scene from a reverse *The Next*
Best Thing. She wanted me as a lover, but now
She wants a woman. I guess a body is not just a body
Coming through the rye. It is 3 p.m. J. D. Salinger opened
"Uncle Wiggily in Connecticut" at 3 p.m. The film
My Foolish Heart based on it is a mess of scenes,

Scenes that so incensed Salinger, he next
Had his will indicate no films be made now or ever.
The plot of *Split Wide Open*. Our bodies. This poem.

Shopping at Williams-Sonoma
"I empty a bottle and I feel a bit free..."
from "Lost in the Supermarket" by The Clash

Replace the shovels and electrical tape
With copper pans, soufflés, and chef's knives.
Descendants of Epicurus, we make
Our way across Union Square's garden
A short walk from Elizabeth Arden.
It is so difficult to be fully alive.

Not the Sears catalog of my mother's youth,
This is something else. To be an epicurean,
To caress the neck of the champagne flute,
To edge the rim of the mouth, press
A nipple to a thimble. The stainless
Utensil feels just a little evil. My shiny mandoline

Exchanges potato and onion for fry
And ring. I know this indulgence must be wrong
And when shopping at Williams-Sonoma I try
To think of Nagasaki and Bangalore
Of the atrocities that came before
I could buy Fleur de Sol plates and dinner tongs.

Yes, yes, I hate war and hate righteousness
Even more, but I need personalized chenille,
A rotary eggbeater, a heat-resistant spoon rest,
And nothing more, except for maybe
Our friends naked on the couch: Fab and Bee,
Grace and Sully, then Fab and Bee with Lucille.

The last thing I want to know is the truth.
The phenomenon of pleasure like art
Is a function of leisure. A kissing booth

At the carnival, its roots in masks,
One thing in place of another, its tasks
Provided by the exuberant luxurious heart.

Perishable Gods

The road at noon, at dark, the mustard field, the field.
The dark barn door, a brown horse behind a white fence
—blindfolded, the white greenhouse, stone's empty gate.
Inhale of air conditioner, hinge of the door, the moon.
The dark barn door, a brown horse behind a white fence,
Warmth at dawn, a memory of kitchen's spicy Malabar.
Inhale of air conditioner, hinge of the door, the moon.
The shape of my coffee cup, half-full, now empty.
Warmth at dawn, a memory of kitchen's spicy Malabar.
I see it, I see her clearly, but I can't remember what was said.
The shape of my coffee cup, half-full, now empty.
A rat climbs the wisteria, finds a bird nest made of wool.
I see it, I see her clearly, but I can't remember what was said.
The bird feeder above the night jasmine is empty.
A rat climbs the wisteria, finds a bird nest made of wool.
A mother covers her boy with night's blanket, a moth flutters.
The bird feeder above the night jasmine is empty.
Green of the pond, the wedding party, the red dragonfly.
A mother covers her boy with night's blanket, a moth flutters.
A bird pecks at crumbs, a housecat's bell.
Green of the pond, the wedding party, the red dragonfly.
Shale stones skip across water, I count 4.
A bird pecks at crumbs, a housecat's bell.
I rest in the sun, air licked cleaned by wind, name it!
Shale stones skip across water, I count 4
Boats, anchored, nosing into wind's squall.
I rest in the sun, air licked cleaned by wind, name it!
She reads the air, a bird responds, I ask "Is it a bird?"
Boats, anchored, nosing into wind's squall.
Lightning over Sand Harbor, a black dog swims ashore.
She reads the air, a bird responds, I ask "Is it a bird?"
Wind chimes in the cricket song, an open window.

Lightning over Sand Harbor, a black dog swims ashore.
I count 4 before purple sky throbs with thunder.
Wind chimes in the cricket song, an open window.
A new wife packs tea in a box marked "perishable gods."
I count 4 before purple sky throbs with thunder.
I see the wing, hear the song, I have no words.
A new wife packs tea in a box marked "perishable gods."
Before the gate the departure hesitates—click.
I see the wing, hear the song, I have no words
—blindfolded, the white greenhouse, stone's empty gate.
Before the gate the departure hesitates—click.
The road at noon, at dark, the mustard field, the field.

The Aquarium at the Potluck

Of note: the California tiger, the glowing zebra,
And the fire-bellied toad. They mingle in giant
Asparagus, they converse on porches of giant
Green fungi fanned out from a plaster tree stump.
In a fire of brain coral the newt sits, stumped.
The party winds down. Our hostess leaves the lights off.
Zebras float in the midst of the thalassic dark.
The evening breeze through the screen door rustles
The paper napkins underneath the ketchup bottle.
The gutted bag of Lay's, torn open by hands ferreting
About conversations, holds the bones of chicken wings.
A shadow of light passes through the room like a shark.
What is it that brings us together, and keeps us apart?
What holds us in our frame, suspended? What art?

Epilogue

To Gerard de Nerval

"I do not ask of God that he should change anything in events themselves, but that he should change me in regard to things, so that I might have the power to create my own universe about me, to govern my dreams instead of enduring them."
—Gerard de Nerval as quoted by Arthur Symons

I

Under how many names did you love the blonde
Adrienne, the one who pecked your cheek
That evening outside the dark château,
The one whose hair you crowned with laurels
As if remembered rather than just met?
There was Jenny Colon, the actress:
The lilt of her smile like the curve of a seashell,
Her white fingers softer than the sand of Nantes.
Then she died too. There were others,
But they did not draw you to the halls
Of the Palais-Royal, leading a lobster
At the end of a snippet of twine. Only Myrtho.
Your reasoning was that it would not bark
And knew the secrets of the sea.

II

Healed, you went east to the badlands
Of Syria to assure us you'd recovered
Your reason. On the steps of the Sheik
Of Lebanon's palace, Salema, a young Druse,
Perpetuated the dream and you almost proposed.
But, seized by an idea or by somnambulism,
You returned to Paris. There you groped
Through filthy alleys after phantoms
You thought filigree which was but twine
Wrapped around three loves, I mean, loaves
Of day-old bread. You lost yourself again
And spent hours, days, infinities
Winding your way back, the writing stopped.

III

You stormed into the *Revue de Paris*
With your latest phantom: a piece of twine
You proclaimed the girdle of Madame de Maintenon
Who performed in *Esther* at Saint Cyr.
Another actress, your mind again decomposed.
The darkness of the streets reeked of fear
But you clung to the twine:
"It is the garter of the Queen of Sheba."
The thin thread of an idea led you
To the rue de la Vieille-Lanterne:
"The Immaculate Conception by geometry…"
Little could the landlord of the penny doss
Who heard the knocking against his window
Guess what drink brought you there.

The May Sarton New Hampshire Poetry Prize

The May Sarton New Hampshire Poetry Prize is named for May Sarton, the renowned novelist, memoirist, poet, and feminist (1912-1995) who lived for many years in Nelson, New Hampshire, not far from Peterborough, home of William L. Bauhan Publishing. In 1967, she approached Bauhan and asked him to publish her book of poetry, *As Does New Hampshire*. She wrote the collection to celebrate the bicentennial of Nelson, and dedicated it to the residents of the town.

May Sarton was a prolific writer of poetry, novels, and perhaps what she is best known for—nonfiction on growing older (*Recovering: A Journal, Journal of Solitude*, among others.) She considered herself a poet, first, though, and in honor of that and to celebrate the centenary of her birth in 2012, Sarah Bauhan, who inherited her father's small publishing company, launched the prize. (www.bauhanpublishing.com/contest)

PAST MAY SARTON WINNERS:

In *The Wreck of Birds*, the first winner of Bauhan Publishing's May Sarton New Hampshire Poetry Prize, Rebecca Givens Rolland embraces an assimilation of internal feeling and thought with circumstances of the natural world and the conflicts and triumphs of our human endeavors. Here, we discover a language that seeks to at once replicate and transcend experiences of loss and disaster, and together with the poet "we hope that such bold fates will not forget us." Even at the speaker's most vulnerable moments, when "Each word we'd spoken / scowls back, mirrored in barrels of wind" these personal poems insist on renewal. With daring honesty and formal skill, *The Wreck of Birds* achieves a revelatory otherness—what Keats called the "soul-making task" of poetry.

—Walter E. Butts, New Hampshire Poet Laureate (2009-2013), and author of *Cathedral of Nervous Horses: New and Selected Poems*, and *Sunday Evening at the Stardust Café*

Rebecca Givens Rolland is a speech-language pathologist and doctoral student at the Harvard Graduate School of Education. Her poetry has previously appeared in journals including *Colorado Review, American Letters & Commentary, Denver Quarterly, Witness,* and the *Cincinnati Review,* and she is the recipient of the Andrew W. Mellon Fellowship, the Clapp Fellowship from Yale University, an Academy of American Poets Prize, and the Dana Award.

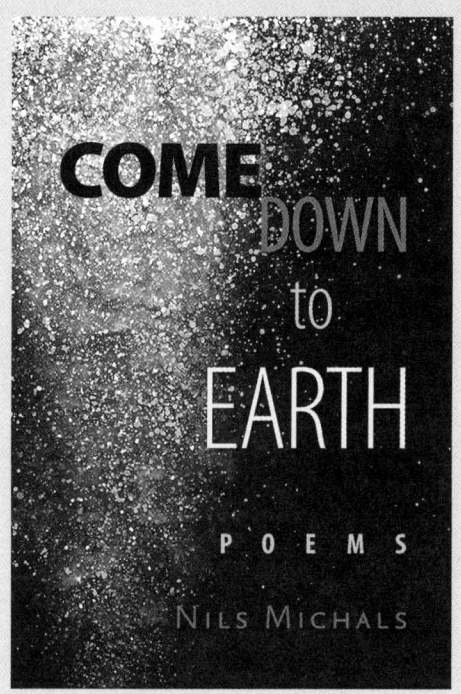

Nils Michals won the second May Sarton New Hampshire Poetry Prize in 2012, and has also written the book *Lure,* which won the Lena-Miles Wever Todd award in 2004. His poetry has been featured in *The Bacon Review, diode, White Whale Review, Bay Poetics, The Laurel Review* and *Sonora Review.* He teaches at the University of Colorado at Boulder.

Nils Michals is alternately healed and wounded by the tension between the timeless machinations of humankind and the modern machinery that lifts us beyond—and plunges us back to—our all-too-human, earthly selves. Supported by minimally narrative, page-oriented forms, his poems transcribe poetry's intangibles—love, loss, hope, a sense of the holy—in a language located somewhere between devotional and raw, but they mourn and celebrate as much of what is surreal in today's news as of what is familiar in the universal mysteries . . . Come Down to Earth is a 'long villa with every door thrown open'"

—Alice B. Fogel, New Hampshire Poet Laureate (2014-2019), and author of *Strange Terrain: A Poetry Handbook for The Reluctant Reader* and *Be That Empty*

Book design by Kirsty Anderson
Typeset in Electra LT
Cover design by Henry James
Manufactured by Versa Press

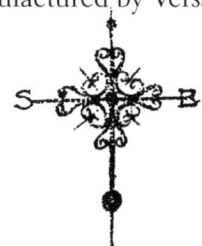